SAVING THE SPOTTED OWL

Zalea's Story

With thanks to all my sources, especially Jasmine,
and my family, especially Freya, Xander and Stefan,
for their input and support. This book is part of our efforts
to leave the world a better place for everyone's children.

Published in Canada and the U.S. by Kids Can Press Ltd.
25 Dockside Drive, Toronto, ON M5A 0B5

Kids Can Press is a Corus Entertainment Inc. company
www.kidscanpress.com

The artwork in this book was rendered digitally.
The text is set in Minion Pro.

Edited by Jennifer Stokes and Kathleen Fraser
Designed by Barb Kelly

Printed and bound in Buji, Shenzhen, China, in 3/2023 by WKT Company

CM 23 0 9 8 7 6 5 4 3 2 1

Library and Archives Canada Cataloguing in Publication

Title: Saving the spotted owl : Zalea's story / written by Nicola Jones ;
illustrations by Alexandra Finkeldey.
Names: Jones, Nicola (Journalist), author. | Finkeldey, Alexandra, illustrator.
Description: Includes index.
Identifiers: Canadiana (print) 20220460485 | Canadiana (ebook) 20220460523 |
ISBN 9781525305559 (hardcover) | ISBN 9781525310713 (EPUB)
Subjects: LCSH: Northern spotted owl — Juvenile literature. |
LCSH: Northern spotted owl — Conservation — Juvenile literature.
Classification: LCC QL696.S83 J66 2023 | DDC j639.97/897 — dc23

Kids Can Press gratefully acknowledges that the land on which our office is located
is the traditional territory of many nations, including the Mississaugas of the Credit, the
Anishnabeg, the Chippewa, the Haudenosaunee and the Wendat peoples, and is now home
to many diverse First Nations, Inuit and Métis peoples.

We thank the Government of Ontario, through Ontario Creates; the Ontario Arts Council; the
Canada Council for the Arts; and the Government of Canada for supporting our publishing activity.

SAVING THE SPOTTED OWL

Zalea's Story

A true story, written
by Nicola Jones

Illustrations by
Alexandra Finkeldey

Kids Can Press

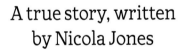

The Fall

One spring day, Zalea fell from her tree.

  She was a baby owl, just three weeks old and not yet able to fly. She landed with a bump on the forest floor, far below her nesting place. She had fallen about as far as if she'd dropped from a seventh-story window.

  This was not good for little Zalea. Tiny and vulnerable, she was in danger of becoming a snack for a passing eagle or a cougar prowling this remote patch of Canadian forest. Her parents couldn't carry their chick back up to the hole in an old-growth tree where they made their home. The most they could do to try to keep their chick safe was to dive-bomb any predators if they came nearby.

But Zalea got lucky. Some wildlife biologists knew that Zalea's parents were nesting in that tree, and they had been visiting now and then to see how the owls were doing. For about a month, they had noticed the father owl bringing a lot of extra food back to the tree. They thought that probably meant there was a chick to feed in the nest.

When the scientists arrived that spring day in 2017, they spotted the little chick sitting on the ground. She was smaller than a soccer ball and looked like an adorable puff of gray fluff. Before the sun set, they made the decision to rescue her.

The biologists carefully picked up the little owl. At that point, the owl chick didn't have a name; no one even knew if it was a boy or a girl. (The team would find out later and then name her Zalea after the beautiful rhododendron bush, an azalea, that grows in British Columbia.) They scooped her up into a cardboard box and put her on the back seat of their truck. Zalea was on her way to her new home.

Out of Danger

That night, Zalea arrived at a special safe place in Langley, British Columbia — a township in Canada close to Vancouver and about two hours' drive from where she fell from her tree. This place was already home to a handful of other owls just like her: northern spotted owls.

The team there wanted to check if she was healthy and that the fall hadn't injured her. One of the biologists, a young woman named Katelyn, helped to measure Zalea and weigh her on a scale. Zalea was 15 cm (6 in.) tall and weighed 400 g (14 oz.), about the same as a can of soda. They looked in her mouth to make sure she wasn't dehydrated and checked to see how chubby and well fed she was. She was given a mouse for her dinner.

Zalea's first night in the Northern Spotted Owl Breeding Centre was the first night she had ever spent inside, away from her home in the wild.

BRITISH COLUMBIA

HOPE

VANCOUVER

COQUITLAM

RICHMOND

Northern Spotted Owl Breeding Centre

CHILLIWACK

LANGLEY

ABBOTSFORD

CANADA

UNITED STATES

The Northern Spotted Owl

SCIENTIFIC NAME: *Strix occidentalis caurina*,
which means "screecher of the northwest."

COLOR:
Northern spotted owls are dark brown with white patches and spots. Their eyes are dark brown.

BODY LENGTH:
An adult owl is about 50 cm (20 in.) long from head to tail, or about one and a half times the length of a school ruler.

WEIGHT: A fully grown owl weighs 500 to 700 g (18 to 25 oz.), or about the same as a loaf of bread.

WINGSPAN: When spread, the wings measure about 1 m (3 ft.) across, or the distance fingertip-to-fingertip of a four-year-old child with arms outstretched.

HABITAT: Northern spotted owls live in old-growth forests from south coastal British Columbia to northern California.

Northern spotted owl

California spotted owl

Mexican spotted owl

COUSINS: Besides the northern spotted owl, there are two other subspecies of spotted owl. The California spotted owl lives only in California and is lighter brown with larger spots. The Mexican spotted owl lives from Utah to Mexico and is the smallest and lightest brown of the three, with the largest white spots.

FOOD: Owls are carnivores, meaning they eat only meat. The northern spotted owl's favorite foods are northern flying squirrels and bushy-tailed woodrats.

Northern flying squirrel

Woodrat

COMPETITION: The barred owl has become more common than the northern spotted owl in its usual territory. The barred owl is larger and has vertical bars, not horizontal spots, on its belly. Its call sounds like "Who cooks for you? Who cooks for you-all?" A spotted owl has a shorter call.

Barred owl

Out in the Woods

The northern spotted owl lives only in the old-growth forests of western North America, from British Columbia to northern California. These forests have been undisturbed by humans, and some of the trees have grown really large over hundreds of years. Even a family of four people might not quite be able to hold hands around the base of one old tree. Northern spotted owls are picky and will make a family only in big trees, usually Douglas firs. They like to find a spot where a branch has broken off and use the resulting hole as a nest.

In Canada, there were once more than a thousand mature northern spotted owls, but as of 2020 there were fewer than just 10 in the wild — perhaps only three.

The big problem for these owls started in the 1980s, when the forests they live in were being cut down for timber. As their nesting sites disappeared, the owls also began to face competition from barred owls, another species that is more aggressive and better at catching food such as mice, woodrats and flying squirrels. With other owls eating their food, and fewer places to live, the spotted owls started to struggle.

People had different feelings about the owls and their plight. Some people were very concerned for the loggers, who needed to make money for their families. They thought the owls could just move to other spots in the forest, and they didn't like restrictions that were put on logging to help the owls. Some even made stickers that read "Save a Logger, Eat an Owl" and put them on their trucks. But others were more concerned about the owls and other animals that make their homes in the old-growth forests.

In the 1990s, laws were passed to help protect the owls, and some logging was stopped. The owls, though, have had a hard time bouncing back.

Even if they don't accidentally fall out of a tree as young chicks the way Zalea did, these owls have difficulty finding a tree to nest in, or a partner to mate with, or enough food to eat. Life is hard in the wild.

8

Endangered

People have a big impact on our planet and the other species that live here. Back in the 1600s, for example, an unusual-looking bird called the dodo met with trouble when sailors arrived on the island of Mauritius. The sailors killed dodos for food and to display their bodies in museums,

Dodo

and rats from the sailors' ships ate the dodos' eggs. Eventually, the dodo became extinct.

Today, we like to think that no one would intentionally kill the last of a species. But people are still driving plants, animals and even bacteria to extinction, often without realizing it, by doing things like cutting down forests to plant farms or build cities. In 2019, for example, the Brazilian blue parrot, Spix's macaw, was declared extinct in the wild. Scientists think that species are becoming extinct far faster now than at any time in the past fifty thousand years.

There are plenty of good reasons to save species — and not just the cute ones, such as pandas, but also less obvious ones, such as insects or plants. Researchers have found that environments are better able to adapt to extreme weather, for example, long periods without any rain, when they are biodiverse. A place with high biodiversity has lots of different species living in it. The more biodiverse a forest or a field is, the better able it is to cope with events like fires or floods, and the better able it is to provide people with resources like food and wood.

The International Union for Conservation of Nature (IUCN) keeps something called the Red List, which tracks how a lot of important species are doing and which ones are threatened. For many species, however, there isn't enough information to say how threatened they are. In the Red List today, all the spotted owls are together listed as "near threatened."

Many countries have their own way of keeping track of and protecting threatened species, including animals, insects and plants. The northern spotted owl is one of Canada's most endangered species.

IUCN Red List Categories

LEAST CONCERN:
At lower risk of extinction

Mimic surgeonfish

NEAR THREATENED:
Would be threatened without ongoing efforts to save them

Bull shark

VULNERABLE:
At risk of global extinction

Hispaniolan yellow tree frog

ENDANGERED:
At great risk of global extinction

Georgia oak

CRITICALLY ENDANGERED:
At most risk of global extinction

Slender-snouted crocodile

EXTINCT:
None left living in the wild, or anywhere at all on Earth

Pinta Island giant tortoise

Safe Haven

In Canada, people had been sounding the alarm about the northern spotted owl for decades. In 2006, a group of scientists decided the best thing to do would be to build a place where the owls could live in safety, while also making sure to preserve enough wild forest for them to call home. The safe place would be a breeding center, a home where biologists help the animals to have families that are as big and healthy as possible.

The Northern Spotted Owl Breeding Program was founded the next year with money from the government of British Columbia. Their breeding center started with just six owls brought in from the wild. It is the only breeding center for spotted owls in the world. Their goal is to help the owls hatch and raise so many healthy chicks that one day they have enough to reintroduce them to the wild. This will be a hard task and it might not work. When the program started, they thought it was the species' best chance for survival in Canada. Now it is their only chance.

The biologists built aviaries for the owls to live in. They are large living spaces enclosed by nets and fences to keep the owls safe from predators. Each owl or owl family has its own space. Large logs are brought in and hollowed out to make suitable nesting spots and are then placed on high ledges. A small group of people keep the owls safe and the aviaries clean. They spend a lot of time cleaning up owl poop.

By the time Zalea arrived in 2017, there were more than a dozen owls living at the center. Some, like Zalea, were brought in because they were in danger in the wild and probably wouldn't make it on their own. Some were injured, or their parents had died. Some were brought in from the United States to help expand the center's community.

Biologist Jasmine McCulligh was at the center when Zalea arrived. Jasmine started as a worker in 2013, and she has been the coordinator there since 2017. Her job is making sure that all the owls are as safe and healthy as possible — and that they have as many chicks as possible.

Biologist Jasmine McCulligh at the Northern Spotted Owl Breeding Centre aviaries.

The Wild Life of a Biologist

Jasmine has always loved animals. As a kid, she was obsessed with dogs. Even when she was in elementary school, she knew she wanted to raise endangered species and release them into the wild. She studied wildlife biology at university.

Zoologist

Before Jasmine came to work with the northern spotted owls, she volunteered for a few weeks at a cheetah breeding program in South Africa. That was an amazing experience for her. Seeing the wild animals in Africa was her childhood dream come true. She says that working with endangered animals inspires both a lot of joy, when the animals thrive, and heartache too, when they can't make a family.

Biologists are scientists who study living things. There are many kinds. Zoologists mostly focus on one particular type of animal, such as birds. Wildlife biologists study the behavior of wild animals and how they interact with their habitats, or the places they live. Botanists study plants. Ecologists study environments — such as the ocean, a forest or a prairie — and how all kinds of animals, insects and plants interact with the air, water and soil.

Wildlife biologist

Wildlife biologists can work with the government, at zoos, with conservation organizations or with rehabilitation centers that try to help injured or sick animals. Some teach or do research at a university. Some, like Jasmine, work with breeding programs.

Wildlife biologists often spend long periods of time outside, in every kind of weather, tramping through swamps or forests to find the animals they study. They may spend time in a laboratory, using special equipment, from basic microscopes to high-tech scientific machines, to examine animals' blood or genes. They also use computers to process their data and look for patterns.

Botanist

Many wildlife biologists study how humans are affecting the planet and its many creatures. For example, as the planet warms because of climate change, some animals are moving into different regions to find food, putting them into contact with new predators or diseases. Some ocean species such as salmon are struggling because of warming waters, overfishing or pollution; salmon are an important food source for whales and other animals as well as for coastal Indigenous communities. Part of the work of many biologists is to study these changes and figure out ways to protect all species from harm.

Ecologist

A New Family

Jasmine knew that Zalea would need to be raised by owls in order to learn how to survive and thrive. The morning after the little owl chick's arrival, she was introduced to her foster parents, Amoré and Sedin. They were a pair of spotted owls with no chicks of their own.

Amoré and Sedin were and still are a very strongly bonded pair. Jasmine often sees them sitting together, grooming each other's feathers.

The biologists opened a small secret door at the back of those owls' nesting spot and carefully put Zalea inside. An owl's nest isn't like a robin's nest. They don't make a structure out of twigs and leaves but instead just find a suitable hole in a log and settle into the hollow. Amoré and Sedin's nest was a hollowed log about 3 m (10 ft.) off the ground.

Everyone on the team held their breath and watched to see what would happen. There were cameras pointed at the nest so they could observe without getting too close. Jasmine knew from experience that most owls will happily adopt new babies, but she was a little anxious that Zalea's foster parents might not accept the strange owl mysteriously arriving in their nest.

Thankfully, Amoré and Sedin seemed very happy to discover they had been gifted a chick. They started to feed and care for her.

The Gang

The Northern Spotted Owl Breeding Program is home to a host of spotted owls, each with its own story.

Shakkai was hit by a car in the 1990s and suffered a broken wing that never quite healed. She never flew again. She was kept elsewhere in captivity for the first few years after she was rescued. She was one of the first owls to arrive at the breeding center in 2007.

Shania was the first chick born at the breeding center, back in 2008. She grew up and had many chicks of her own.

Zalea's foster mom, **Amoré**, was brought to the center in 2010. She came as a fledgling with her brother. They were born to a pair of wild owls in a British Columbia forest.

Zalea's foster father, **Sedin**, was born from the first artificially incubated spotted owl egg in the world. He was born at the breeding center in 2012.

Skalula is a very special owl for Jasmine. Jasmine thinks of this little owl as her firstborn, because her egg was laid on Jasmine's birthday. *Skalula* means "owl" in several Interior Salish languages spoken by some of the First Nations peoples living in British Columbia.

Growing Up

Just a few days after being introduced to Amoré and Sedin, Zalea left her new nest for the first time.

She hooked her beak onto the edge of the nest stump, climbed up the sides with her feet and wobbled onto a nearby branch. She spent the next week exploring close to her nest and using the branches to climb around. As her muscles got stronger, she tried to fly. At first it was just a few short swoops, close to the ground. There were some crash landings, but she was always able to climb back up to safety. After a few weeks of test flights, her muscles got stronger and her skills developed.

By the time Zalea was four months old, she looked all grown-up and could fly just as well as her foster parents. Now that she was old enough, Jasmine gave Zalea a space of her own. Sedin and Amoré were no longer being pestered with constant demands for food and attention.

About a year later, in the spring, it was time for the owls at the center to begin choosing their mates and getting ready to lay eggs. Was Zalea ready to start a family?

Zalea seemed eager. She started to lay eggs, a sign that she was ready to have a chick. But without a partner to fertilize the eggs, those eggs couldn't develop into babies.

Jasmine and her team decided to let Zalea start by being a foster mom to a young barred owl chick so she could practice raising a baby. Zalea was a natural. She protected the chick and provided food for it with just a bit of help from the biologists. Being a single owl mom is really only possible in a place like a breeding center, where people provide food. In the wild, Zalea would have needed a partner to go hunting for her and her chick while she sat by the nest.

A year later, Jasmine's team introduced Zalea to Einstein — an older male spotted owl. At first, Einstein was not that enamored of Zalea. But Zalea was persistent, and she kept pursuing Einstein until he changed his mind.

Owl Courtship

Spotted owls have their own way of starting a family. In February, right around the time when humans are celebrating Valentine's Day, the male owl starts to bring gifts to the female. Instead of chocolates, he brings dead mice. That might not sound good to you, but to an owl it's a fantastic dinner, and it shows the female that the male will make a good provider when their chicks arrive. If the female accepts the food, that means she accepts the male as a partner and mate. The male can then fertilize an egg forming inside the female.

If they do this at the right time, then when the female lays her eggs in March, baby chicks might grow inside them.

A Family of Her Own

That spring, Zalea laid two eggs and then, later, two more. That is a lot of eggs for such a young mom.

Jasmine and her team watched with excitement as Zalea carefully sat on her first two eggs to keep them warm. Then they did something that might seem very odd. They waited until Zalea got off the nest to go stretch her wings, and while she was gone, they carefully removed her eggs from the nest and left fake eggs in place of the real ones. Zalea didn't even notice the switch when she returned.

The fake eggs are little electronic devices the same size and color as real spotted owl eggs. They have sensors for temperature and humidity (the amount of water in the air) inside them, so Jasmine and her team can learn more about the natural conditions inside an owl nest.

The team swapped Zalea's eggs, as they do for all the owl moms, for a good reason. They wanted Zalea to think her eggs weren't hatching so she would lay some more. That would mean that Zalea's family had a chance to be twice as big as it would be in the wild. It worked. Zalea laid two more eggs. The biologists replaced those with fake eggs, too.

What about her real eggs? Don't worry. Jasmine and her team were taking extremely good care of them. The biologists placed all of Zalea's eggs into a special machine called an incubator.

In each incubator, the temperature, humidity and rotation can be changed to match what each egg needs. The incubator is monitored closely, and if an alarm goes off to say that something is broken or wrong, the biologists race to fix the situation. Each egg is precious and is given the very best care possible.

Incubating Eggs

Chicken farmers know a lot about how to incubate eggs. Most of the chicken for sale at bigger grocery stores comes from large farms that raise chickens for meat. To get so many chickens, they use huge incubators that can protect and hatch thousands of chicks at a time.

Some people may use an incubator to raise just a handful of chicks. It can be exciting to watch baby chicks hatch and grow. But be warned: having chickens is a big responsibility, and incubating eggs can be tricky.

Some kids at a daycare center in Pemberton, British Columbia, were lucky enough to see this for themselves. One of the daycare workers was keeping chickens at home. She brought in six eggs laid by a hen (a chicken mom) living with a rooster (a chicken dad).

The center bought a small incubator and popped the eggs inside. It had all the right temperature and humidity sensors and controls needed for incubating chickens. The incubator kept the conditions for the eggs just right because one degree too warm or too cold can stop a chick from growing. It helped them make sure there was exactly the right amount of moisture in the air. It also rotated the eggs automatically. The machine acted just like a good mother.

Chickens don't take as long to hatch as northern spotted owls do. After about 21 days, a little chick started pecking its way out of one of the eggs. The kids were so excited!

The hardest part, said the adults at the daycare, was figuring out what to do with the live chicks once they were born. Taking care of a chicken is harder than incubating an egg.

Hatchlings

A few days after each of Zalea's eggs was put into the incubator, Jasmine's team shined a flashlight on it to see what was going on inside. This is called candling. Eggshells are thin enough that, with a light, you can see a little of what is inside them. Zalea's first egg showed no hint of a chick growing inside. But the other three eggs showed the first sign of life: a tiny embryo of a baby chick.

Sadly, one of these embryos stopped growing inside its egg. No one really knows why. But the other two kept developing normally.

After a week, the biologists spotted tiny heartbeats and a web of blood vessels in each egg. These blood vessels let the developing chicks breathe by pulling in oxygen from outside the shell, a bit like how an umbilical cord works for a human baby.

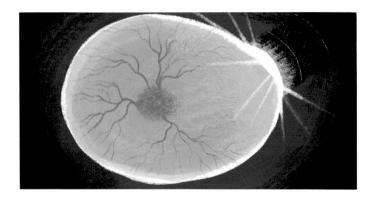
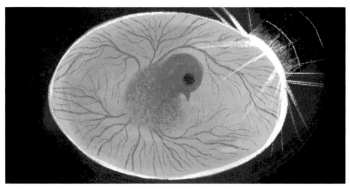

After about a month, the chicks inside absorbed the blood vessels into their bodies and got ready to hatch.

At this point, Jasmine and members of her team started to take turns sleeping at the center. They needed to watch the eggs all day and night to be sure that all the conditions were just right for the chicks.

After 32 days, the chick inside one of Zalea's eggs pipped. That means it made a small crack in the eggshell and took its first breath of fresh air. The biologists could hear the chick peeping inside the egg. Over the next three days, the crack grew bigger and bigger, eventually forming a zigzag pattern around the egg.

Finally, the chick emerged. It was a teeny, tiny, featherless creature.

A little while later, Zalea's second egg began to hatch and another chick emerged.

Zalea was now a mother to two chicks, making her the youngest mother in the history of the breeding center. Everyone was very proud of her. Jasmine and her team named the chicks Georgia and Skagit.

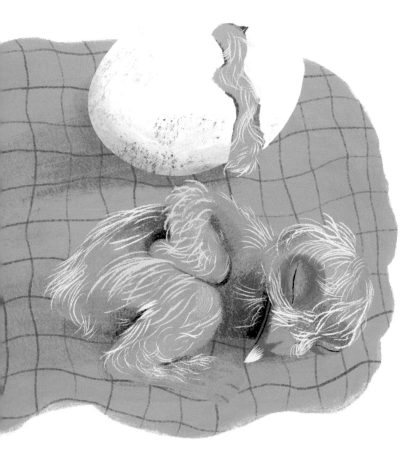

The Life of a Spotted Owl

1 month old
Chicks stay in nest. Father owl hunts and mother feeds chicks.

2 months old
Chicks fledge and leave nest for short flights.

In early spring, a female owl lays one to three eggs. After a month, chicks start to hatch.

3 to 4 months old
Young owls grow adult feathers and can fly but still rely on parents for food.

5 to 6 months old
Fully grown, they can hunt on their own.

The average northern spotted owl lives about 15 years in the wild if it survives its first year. Shakkai lived in captivity to the grand old age of 25 years.

Over a lifetime, female owls can have 5 to 20 chicks in the wild, and more in captivity.

1 year old
Owls are ready to find a partner and have their own families.

In the fall, young owls leave to find their own territory.

Tricky Business

In her first year with a partner, Zalea had laid four eggs but produced only two chicks. This is not unusual. Owls in the wild will lay more than one egg in the hope that at least one survives, since not every egg turns out just right. Having a chick is a tricky business.

Trouble can arrive after a chick emerges from the egg, too. For example, the same spring that Zalea first arrived at the center, a tiny little chick called Dante became very sick just three days after hatching.

Because there are so few northern spotted owls, and biologists don't have a lot of experience raising them, it was hard to know what to do. Jasmine was very worried. She spent all night cradling Dante in her palm and trying to feed him medicine through a tiny medicine dropper. He would grimace at the taste, just like a human baby might. On the fourth day of intensive care, he finally started to get his appetite back. He eventually grew up into a strong owl.

Zalea's chicks seemed healthy. One of Skagit's legs looked a bit crooked in the first few days of life, so Jasmine and her colleagues made a little leg brace for him out of cardboard, a paper clip and an elastic band. They had done that for other chicks before. Skagit's leg straightened right out.

Skagit needed a little leg brace to help straighten his leg.

Dante needed medicine from a tiny medicine dropper.

When the chicks are tiny, Jasmine's team does its best to make them feel they are being raised in a forest, just as they would be in the wild. The chicks don't open their eyes for a while, so they can't see that they are in a laboratory. The biologists don't speak around them and instead play recordings of sounds of the forest and owl calls. They sometimes give them a little stuffed toy owl, or even just a sponge, to cuddle with, until they go to live with other owls. If they have brothers or sisters, they grow up together. The team wants the owls to have the very best care possible, while limiting their contact with people.

Growing Numbers

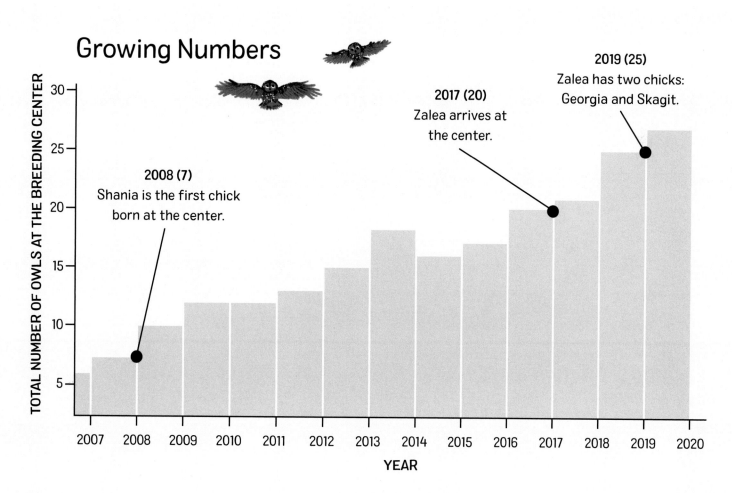

2008 (7)
Shania is the first chick born at the center.

2017 (20)
Zalea arrives at the center.

2019 (25)
Zalea has two chicks: Georgia and Skagit.

TOTAL NUMBER OF OWLS AT THE BREEDING CENTER

YEAR

Back to the Wild

Jasmine's hope is that one day there will be enough northern spotted owl chicks, made strong and healthy by their care at the breeding center, to create a thriving population in the wild.

In order for the released owls to thrive, there needs to be a good, safe place for them to live. In British Columbia, the provincial government manages more than 363 000 hectares (897 000 acres) for spotted owl recovery. (That's two-thirds the size of Prince Edward Island or almost the size of Rhode Island.) Some of this habitat still has a lot of maturing to do before it becomes old growth, but other areas would already make great homes for northern spotted owls.

The first step on this path was taken in the summer of 2022, when three male owls were brought to the woods and released into the wild.

To do this, the team first built aviaries in a patch of protected forest in the Fraser Canyon, where spotted owls used to live. The aviaries allowed the owls to get used to the new environment and prove they could hunt live prey. Before opening the doors to the wild, the team also checked that there were no wildfires or competing barred owls in the area. They did all this in collaboration with the Spuzzum Nation, a local First Nation.

These owls will need to fend for themselves, hunt their own prey and compete against other animals for nesting sites and food. They will have to watch out for predators, such as the great horned owl and northern goshawk. They also have to be cautious of humans, even though humans were helping them at the center.

The team will track these three male owls using electronic tags and by listening for them in the forest. They will make sure that the owls continue to find food.

In the coming years, the plan is to release more owls, maybe as many as 20 every year. Eventually, the team hopes that the owls will pair up and have families in the wild.

There are still many challenges. Logging is still allowed in some of these areas. And it can be dangerous for the owls to get from one patch of good forest to another. Traveling through logged forests makes it hard for the owls to find food, and there is no place to hide from predators. Many people are working hard to make sure there is enough protected habitat for these owls to thrive.

Breeding Centers

Breeding centers around the world have been used to bring other species back from the brink of extinction.

California Condor

In 1987, there were fewer than 30 of the giant, vulture-like condors left in California. They were almost extinct, thanks to the problems they faced in the wild, including lead poisoning from eating animals that had been shot by hunters. Then, as part of a condor recovery program, the last birds were captured and brought to breeding centers. Eventually, the centers started releasing birds back into the wild. Everyone celebrated when the thousandth new California condor chick since the program started hatched in 2019. They are still critically endangered, but there are now more than 300 California condors flying free in the wild.

CALIFORNIA, UNITED STATES

TASMANIA, AUSTRALIA

Tasmanian Devil

In Australia, a meat-eating marsupial called the Tasmanian devil faces a nasty disease: a face cancer that is infectious. (Marsupial mothers carry their young in pouches. A kangaroo is another marsupial.) The number of Tasmanian devils has gone down in some places as much as 95 percent since the 1990s, making the animal endangered. But now there are dozens of breeding centers to help boost their numbers. Some of the devils born in captivity were released onto a disease-free island in 2012. There were 28 to begin with and now there are more than 100 on the island. This has caused other problems, though, as the island devils have eaten a lot of local birds and penguins.

Mongolian Wild Horse

Przewalski's horse is a small, stocky horse that traditionally lived in the high, dry grasslands of Mongolia, a country between Russia and China. This Mongolian wild horse, which has never been tamed, is called *takhi*, which means "spirit" in Mongolian. It went extinct in the wild in the 1960s. Scientists have taken some Mongolian horses from zoos and breeding centers and reintroduced them to the wild. From the first 16 horses brought back in 1992, today there are hundreds running free.

MONGOLIA

HAWAII, UNITED STATES

Hawaiian Crow

The 'Alalā is the only surviving crow species in Hawaii. It is revered by Indigenous peoples on those Hawaiian islands, but sadly it became extinct in the wild. Thanks to a successful breeding program, more than 100 birds have been born in captivity. The program started releasing them in 2016, but the crows faced many predator hawks and did not start their own families in the wild. Biologists are still working to find a way for the crows to survive by themselves without extra help.

A Growing Family

Jasmine and her team took good care of Zalea's chicks, weighed them, and took blood samples to determine if they were boys or girls.

Just like a human parent, Jasmine kept such a close eye on the chicks in their early days that she could even tell when the tiny baby birds started to breathe differently. Every time a chick pooped, a biologist would take a look at it to see if the color and texture were healthy. They kept Georgia and Skagit comfortable for 10 days before returning them to a nest in the aviary.

Georgia was given to foster parents who didn't have a chick of their own. Skagit — named after the Skagit Valley, which is an area in British Columbia that used to be home to wild northern spotted owls — was given to his biological parents, Zalea and Einstein. Zalea was now being a mom for one of her own baby chicks.

Jasmine and her team use cameras to watch baby owls as they grow up in the nest and learn to walk and fly. Like human toddlers, owls like to eat and explore with their mouths. The team saw Skagit stealing food right out of Zalea's beak. And they once spotted Georgia eating a slimy black slug.

Zalea's chicks have grown up to be happy and healthy owls with their own personalities. Jasmine says that Skagit always looks a little angry. He has what looks to us humans like a glare on his face. He is fairly calm, Jasmine says, and has his favorite spots where he likes to chill out. Georgia, on the other hand, is feisty like her mother. She is a bold and confident owl, says Jasmine.

As a young, healthy owl, Zalea still has a lot of years of motherhood ahead of her. Together, Jasmine, the other biologists, Zalea and her chicks, and all the other owls at the center might help to save the northern spotted owl in British Columbia.

Glossary

aviaries: large structures built with fences and netting to hold birds

biodiverse: having a variety of different types of life in a given place, including plants, animals and tiny bugs and microbes. Rainforests are very biodiverse.

biologists: scientists who study living things, such as animals, plants and environments

botanists: scientists who study plants

breeding centers: places where biologists help animals to have families that are as big and healthy as possible

candling: shining a flashlight on an egg to see what is going on inside

captivity: not the wild; a place maintained by people

carnivores: animals that eat only meat

climate change: the way the planet is getting warmer and the weather is changing because of human activities such as releasing pollution into the air

conservation organizations: groups that try to restore, protect and maintain natural populations of plants or animals

courtship: the practice of attracting a mate

dehydrated: suffering from not having enough water to drink

ecologists: scientists who study environments — such as the ocean, a forest or a prairie — and how all kinds of animals, insects and plants interact with the air, water and soil

embryo: the first stage of life in an unborn baby

endangered: at great risk of global extinction. "Critically endangered" means at most risk of global extinction.

extinct: none left living anywhere at all on Earth. "Extinct in the wild" means none left living in the wild, but some may live in zoos or other managed places.

fertilize: when a male contributes to a female egg so that a baby can grow

fledge: to leave the nest at the right time as a baby bird. A "fledgling" is a baby bird that has left the nest and is just learning how to fly.

grooming: the practice of cleaning fur or feathers. Animals do this for themselves and, sometimes, for other animals.

habitat: a type of place that an animal likes to live in, such as a forest, desert or lake

hatch: to emerge from an egg

hen: a female chicken. Only a hen lays eggs.

humidity: the amount of water in the air

incubate: to control conditions like temperature and humidity to help raise an egg or young baby

incubator: a machine that controls conditions such as temperature and humidity to help raise an egg or young baby. An egg or baby that is kept in perfect conditions and cared for in a machine rather than by a mother is artificially incubated.

Indigenous peoples: the earliest inhabitants of a place. Indigenous peoples have ancestral ties to the land and distinct cultures developed throughout history.

intensive care: when an animal or person receives a lot of care and medical attention

International Union for Conservation of Nature (IUCN): an international organization that works to help conserve nature

logging: the practice of cutting down trees to use the wood. "Loggers" are the people who do the work of logging.

marsupial: a kind of mammal that, after being born, continues to grow in its mother's pouch

mate: a partner in raising a family, or the act of trying to make a baby

mature: grown-up

monogamous: when an animal pairs with just one partner for life

old-growth forest: a very old forest that remains undisturbed by people. In British Columbia, Canada, "old-growth trees" are more than 100 to 200 years old. Some are 1000 years old.

pip: when a chick makes a small crack in an eggshell and takes its first breath

predator: an animal that naturally eats another animal

Red List: a list maintained by the International Union for Conservation of Nature (IUCN) to keep track of the conservation status of different species of plants, animals and more

rehabilitation centers: groups that try to help injured or sick animals, with the intent of returning them to the wild

rooster: a male chicken

species: a type of plant, animal or other organism that can reproduce or have babies with other members of that group. A "subspecies" is a specific group within a species that is distinctive because of how it looks or where it lives.

talon: a bird's toenail

territory: a patch of land that an animal considers its own, to live in and hunt food in

threatened: at risk of harm. "Near threatened," according to the IUCN, means a species that is threatened without ongoing efforts to save it.

thrive: to live and grow in a healthy way

timber: wood that has been cut and prepared for use as a building material

vulnerable: at risk of harm; in need of special care or support. The IUCN uses this word to describe species threatened with global extinction.

wildlife biologists: scientists who study the behavior of wild animals and how they interact with their habitats or the places they live

zoologists: scientists who tend to focus on one particular kind of animal, such as birds

Author's Note

Many thanks to Jasmine McCulligh, facility coordinator of the Northern Spotted Owl Breeding Program, for her help in putting together the stories, pictures and scientific information in this book. Without her, this project would not have been possible, but any mistakes that might have slipped in remain my own. This book is not a representation of the official views of the Northern Spotted Owl Breeding Program or the provincial government of British Columbia, Canada.

Any profits from the sale of this book will be split between the Northern Spotted Owl Breeding Program and the author.

— Nicola Jones

Do More and Read More

The Northern Spotted Owl Breeding Program allows you to adopt an egg or an owl. For a small fee, you can get updates and photos. Find out more about the Northern Spotted Owl Breeding Program and view their live webcams at www.nsobreedingprogram.com and www.facebook.com/nsobreedingprogram. On Instagram find them at @nsobreeding.

Index